CORE LIBRARY OF US STATES

ARKANSAS

BY A. R. CARSER
CONTENT CONSULTANT
John A. Kirk, PhD
George W. Donaghey Distinguished Professor of History
University of Arkansas at Little Rock

Core Library
An Imprint of Abdo Publishing
abdobooks.com

abdobooks.com

Published by Abdo Publishing, a division of ABDO, PO Box 398166, Minneapolis, Minnesota 55439. Copyright © 2023 by Abdo Consulting Group, Inc. International copyrights reserved in all countries. No part of this book may be reproduced in any form without written permission from the publisher. Core Library™ is a trademark and logo of Abdo Publishing.

Printed in the United States of America, North Mankato, Minnesota.
052022
092022

Cover Photos: Shutterstock Images, map and icons, mockingbird; Shane Sabin/Shutterstock Images, deer
Interior Photos: Damon Shaw/Shutterstock Images, 4–5; Shutterstock Images, 8, 13 (flag), 13 (fiddle), 13 (pecan), 26–27, 29; Red Line Editorial, 9 (Arkansas), 9 (USA); Jessie Tarbox Beals/The New York Historical Society/Archive Photos/Getty Images, 10–11; Steve Byland/Shutterstock Images, 13 (bird); S. C. Colbing/Shutterstock Images, 13 (flower); Photo 12/Universal Images Group/Getty Images, 15, 43; Desi Drew Photography/Shutterstock Images, 20–21, 45; Ashley Elizabeth Martin/Shutterstock Images, 24; Ian G. Dagnall/Alamy, 31; Denis Tangney Jr./iStockphoto, 34–35; Andy Altenburger/Icon Sportswire/Getty Images, 37; Michael Ochs Archives/Getty Images, 39

Editor: Katharine Hale
Series Designer: Joshua Olson

Library of Congress Control Number: 2021951384

Publisher's Cataloging-in-Publication Data

Names: Carser, A. R., author.
Title: Arkansas / by A. R. Carser
Description: Minneapolis, Minnesota : Abdo Publishing, 2023 | Series: Core library of US states | Includes online resources and index.
Identifiers: ISBN 9781532197451 (lib. bdg.) | ISBN 9781098270216 (ebook)
Subjects: LCSH: U.S. states--Juvenile literature. | Southeastern States--Juvenile literature. | Arkansas--History--Juvenile literature. | Physical geography--United States--Juvenile literature.
Classification: DDC 976.7--dc23

Population demographics broken down by race and ethnicity come from the 2019 census estimate. Population totals come from the 2020 census.

CONTENTS

CHAPTER ONE
The Natural State 4

CHAPTER TWO
History of Arkansas 10

CHAPTER THREE
Geography and Climate 20

CHAPTER FOUR
Resources and Economy 26

CHAPTER FIVE
People and Places 34

Important Dates........................ 42

Stop and Think........................ 44

Glossary................................ 46

Online Resources 47

Learn More 47

Index 48

About the Author..................... 48

CHAPTER ONE

THE NATURAL STATE

At Kyles Landing, a family puts on their life jackets. They slide their kayaks into the river. Birds sing in the trees. The sound of the rushing water fills the family's ears.

They are going to camp along the Buffalo National River. The river winds through northern Arkansas. This region is the family's ancestral home. They are members of the Osage Nation. The US government forced their ancestors out of Arkansas in the 1800s.

People can kayak and canoe down the Buffalo River in Arkansas.

ENDANGERED SPECIES IN ARKANSAS

From rivers and lakes to forests and plains, Arkansas offers lots of habitats. The state is home to 37 threatened and endangered species. If visitors are lucky, they may spot an Ozark big-eared bat flying at dusk. They may spy an eastern black rail bird along the shore. Very lucky visitors may find an Ozark hellbender salamander hiding under a rock in a stream. It is one of the largest salamanders in the world.

The family now lives in eastern Oklahoma. But today they are home on the Buffalo. They begin their 5.7-mile (9.2-km) journey to Erbie Ford. In some places, the narrow river snakes through sandstone canyons. In others, trees line the shore. The family spots a group of white-tailed deer drinking along the shoreline. An American mink slinks through the underbrush. A bald eagle perches on a dead tree overhanging the river. The eagle scans the water, hunting for fish. Soon the family will fish for their own lunch.

LAY OF THE LAND

Arkansas is in the South Central US region. Missouri borders Arkansas to the north. Oklahoma and Texas are to the west. The Mississippi River makes up the state's eastern border. Across the river are Tennessee and Mississippi. Louisiana borders Arkansas to the south.

Arkansas is mostly a rural state. But it does have important cities. Little Rock is the capital

PERSPECTIVES

DALE BUMPERS WHITE RIVER

The Dale Bumpers White River National Wildlife Refuge is in eastern Arkansas. This area is an important habitat for migrating birds. Yellow prothonotary warblers and colorful wood ducks visit the refuge in spring and summer. The refuge is home to the only native black bears in Arkansas. It is named after former Arkansas governor and US Senator Dale Bumpers. Bumpers fought to protect 91,000 acres (37,000 ha) of wilderness in Arkansas. The US Fish and Wildlife Service (FWS) dedicated the refuge to Bumpers in 2014. At the ceremony, FWS Director Dan Ashe said of Bumpers, "He is a giant among conservationists and a visionary who . . . set aside Arkansas's last wild places."

The Texarkana building that houses the post office and courthouse is on the state line.

of Arkansas. It is in the middle of the state. Fayetteville is in the northwestern corner of Arkansas. It is home to the University of Arkansas. Texarkana is in southwestern Arkansas. It is on the border with Texas. The state line splits the city in half. But even in Arkansas's cities, nature is close by. That is why Arkansas is called the Natural State.

MAP OF ARKANSAS

Study the map below. What do you notice about the locations of Arkansas's cities? How does this map help you understand Arkansas's geography?

CHAPTER TWO

HISTORY OF ARKANSAS

The first people to live in modern-day Arkansas arrived approximately 30,000 years ago. Over the centuries, several peoples called the region home. This included the Woodland people between 600 BCE and 900 CE and the Mississippian people after 900 CE. Caddo people farmed lands in the southwest region of present-day Arkansas. The Wahzhazhe (Osage) people hunted in the northwest region. Ogaxpa (Quapaw) people lived

Many settlers came to Arkansas for its rich soil. By 1900, 1.3 million people lived in the state.

along the Mississippi, Arkansas, and Ouachita rivers in eastern Arkansas.

In 1541 Spanish explorer Hernando de Soto was the first European to encounter the American Indian peoples of modern-day Arkansas. French explorer Henri de Tonti founded the first permanent European trading post in eastern Arkansas in 1686. French traders and American Indians traded goods at Arkansas Post. France created Louisiana Colony in 1699. The colony eventually extended into present-day Arkansas. White colonists traded furs and other goods with American Indian communities. In 1803 the United States bought the land from France in the Louisiana Purchase. The American Indian peoples who had lived there since long before Europeans arrived had no say in the deal.

FROM TERRITORY TO STATE

The rich soil of southern Arkansas attracted cotton farmers from eastern states. Some of these farmers brought enslaved Black people with them to work

ARKANSAS
QUICK FACTS

Each US state has its own unique culture. How do Arkansas's state nickname and symbols represent its culture? Did you find any of Arkansas's state symbols surprising?

Abbreviation: AR
Nickname: The Natural State
Motto: *Regnat populus* (The people rule)
Date of statehood: June 15, 1836
Capital: Little Rock
Population: 3,011,524
Area: 53,179 square miles (137,732 sq km)

STATE SYMBOLS

State bird
Northern mockingbird

State musical instrument
Fiddle

State flower
Apple blossom

State nut
Pecan

on large farms called plantations. On July 4, 1819, Arkansas became a US territory. At that time, a territory was a region that the United States claimed but was not populated enough to become a state. In 1820 Missouri entered the United States as a state. Missouri's statehood was hotly debated. To make it possible, Congress created a compromise that shaped Arkansas's future. In Missouri and future southern states, slavery would be legal. In northern states, it would be illegal. This decision about slavery was called the Missouri Compromise.

Beginning in the 1830s, the US government forcibly relocated American Indian peoples from their homelands. The government removed approximately 100,000 Cherokee and Choctaw people from their homes in the southeast United States. It forced them to march west to Indian Territory in Oklahoma. Approximately 15,000 people lost their lives on the journey. This journey is called the Trail of Tears. Four routes on the Trail of Tears passed through Arkansas.

The Battle of Pea Ridge was one of many American Civil War battles fought in Arkansas.

Arkansas became the twenty-fifth state on June 15, 1836. At that time Congress took away American Indian peoples' land rights in the state. Today just 1 percent of Arkansas's population is American Indian. No federally recognized tribes are found within Arkansas's borders.

THE CIVIL WAR

Because of the Missouri Compromise, Arkansas entered the United States as a slave state. The issue of slavery eventually led to the American Civil War (1861–1865). The Southern states seceded from the United States, called the Union, to create the Confederacy. Arkansas joined the Confederacy in May 1861. The economic

THE ELAINE MASSACRE

In 1919 Black sharecroppers in Elaine tried forming a union. They wanted better pay and treatment from white farmers. Armed sharecroppers stood guard. A group of white people fired into the church where the meeting was held. In the gunfight that followed, a white person was killed. White people said the sharecroppers were planning a violent uprising. They came from nearby towns to attack Black people in Elaine, regardless of whether the victims had been at the meeting. Historians believe more than 200 Black people were killed in the violence. None of the white perpetrators were charged with crimes.

system of Arkansas and other Confederate states relied on enslaved people's labor. Dozens of battles between Confederate and Union troops occurred in Arkansas. The Confederacy lost the war in 1865. Arkansas rejoined the United States on June 22, 1868.

After the Civil War, slavery was abolished. White landowners leased land to Black and white farm laborers called sharecroppers and tenant farmers.

These farmers paid rent to the landowner in crops or cash. Many formerly enslaved people became trapped in debt under this system.

To maintain racial segregation after the Civil War, Arkansas and other Southern states passed Jim Crow Laws. These laws restricted the movement, education, labor, and political power of Black people. Many Black Arkansans left the state because of these laws and lack of jobs.

PERSPECTIVES
SOUTHERN TENANT FARMERS' UNION

Landowners often took advantage of the sharecroppers and tenant farmers who worked their fields. Some failed to pay farmers what they were owed. Others kicked farmers off their land without paying them. Black and white farmers and activists created the Southern Tenant Farmers' Union in 1934. Union member Isaac Shaw explained how landlords often pitted Black farmers against white ones. "The landlord is always [between] us, beatin' us, starvin' us and makin' us fight each other. There ain't but one way for us to get him where he can't help himself and that's for us to get together and stay together."

In 1929 the Great Depression started. Around the same time, a drought hit Arkansas. Farmers did not plant as much and did not need as many workers. Displaced Black and white farmers looked elsewhere for work. Some relocated to towns and cities in Arkansas, while others left the state entirely.

DESEGREGATING ARKANSAS

In 1954 the US Supreme Court ruled in *Brown v. Board of Education of Topeka* that segregated schools were illegal. States, including Arkansas, had to desegregate their schools.

The governor of Arkansas, Orval Faubus, refused to comply with the ruling. On September 2, 1957, Faubus ordered the Arkansas National Guard to Little Rock Central High School. The state troops prevented Black students from entering. On September 25, 1957, the US government sent federal troops to allow nine Black students to attend Central High School. These students became known as the Little Rock Nine.

GOVERNMENT

Arkansas's government today has three branches. The governor heads the executive branch. The governor serves a four-year term. The state legislature is called the General Assembly. It has two chambers: the Senate and the House of Representatives. Arkansas's judicial branch interprets its laws. The system includes city and district courts, a Court of Appeals, and a state Supreme Court.

FURTHER EVIDENCE

Chapter Two discusses American Indian removal. What was one of the author's main points? What evidence is included to support this point? Read the article at the website below. Does the information on the website support the author's point? Does it present new evidence?

TRAIL OF TEARS
abdocorelibrary.com/arkansas

CHAPTER THREE

GEOGRAPHY AND CLIMATE

Arkansas has hot, humid summers and mild winters. Ice and snow can occur in the winter months. Cool, dry air rolls east off the western mountains and collides with the warm, humid air rising from the eastern plains. This causes severe thunderstorms and flooding between March and May.

MOUNTAINS

The Ozark Mountains stretch from Missouri into northwest Arkansas. They are primarily

The Buffalo River flows through the Ozark Mountains.

PERSPECTIVES
LOGGING IN NATIONAL FORESTS

The US Forest Service manages the Ozark-Saint Francis National Forests and the Ouachita National Forest. It works with companies to harvest timber from the national forests. The Forest Service does this to remove fuel for potential wildfires and improve the health of the forests. Selling timber also helps the Forest Service fund its programs. Harvesting timber in national forests is controversial. Some conservationists argue that forests do not need human intervention to remain healthy. They worry commercial logging in the forests will harm wildlife and habitats.

sandstone and limestone. Water dissolves limestone over time, forming caves and rocky features such as ridges and bluffs. Many Arkansas rivers start in the Ozarks, including the White River and Buffalo River. In the western part of the state, the Arkansas River forms a valley between the Ozark and Ouachita Mountains. The Ouachita Mountains stretch from the Oklahoma border to Little Rock.

These mountains create a long ridge that travels east to west.

Black bears are one of the largest mammals found in the mountains. Three endangered bat species live in the caves in Arkansas's mountains. They are the Ozark big-eared bat, the gray bat, and the Indiana bat.

IVORY-BILLED WOODPECKER

In 2005 researchers canoed along the White River in central Arkansas. They were looking for an ivory-billed woodpecker. Scientists thought this large woodpecker was extinct. One had not been spotted since the mid-1900s. But these scientists thought they spotted one. They captured a few seconds of video of the bird but no photographs. Many scientists tried finding proof of the bird's existence. But they were unsuccessful. In 2021 the ivory-billed woodpecker was officially ruled as extinct.

PLAINS

Southern Arkansas is part of the West Gulf Coastal Plain. Approximately 50 million years ago, the Gulf of Mexico covered this region. Gradually the water receded, leaving behind flat and gently rolling plains.

Minerals from dripping water create the formations of Blanchard Springs Caverns.

In eastern Arkansas the Mississippi River creates the Mississippi Alluvial Plain. Over time the river has added minerals to the soil that make it ideal for farming. Other parts of the plain are too wet for agriculture. These wetlands create habitats for birds.

PROTECTED NATURAL WONDERS

Sections of the Ozark Mountains are part of the Ozark-Saint Francis National Forests. This area features the tallest mountain in Arkansas, Mount Magazine. It is 2,753 feet (839 m) tall.

The national forest also features the Blanchard Springs Caverns. The white Ozark blind salamander spends its entire life in the caves. Bats, crayfish, and insects also live there.

Hot Springs National Park is near Ouachita National Forest. The water in the springs absorbs heat and minerals from underground. It is cooled and piped into bathhouses where people can soak in it. Arkansas's natural wonders have something for everyone.

EXPLORE ONLINE

Chapter Three covers the geography, plants, and animals of Arkansas, including bats. The article at the website below goes into more depth on this topic. Does the article answer any of the questions you had about bats?

BAT JUNIOR RANGER ACTIVITY PAGE

abdocorelibrary.com/arkansas

CHAPTER FOUR
RESOURCES AND ECONOMY

Several industries rely on Arkansas's natural resources. The agricultural industry takes advantage of the state's fertile soil. The forest products industry relies on Arkansas's healthy forests. Tourists visit the state for its natural beauty and thriving cities.

AGRICULTURE AND FORESTS

Poultry farming is the leading agricultural industry in Arkansas. Farmers raise chickens

Raising poultry is a major industry in Arkansas.

PERSPECTIVES
CONTRACT FARMING

Some farmers work directly with poultry companies. The companies provide farmers with chicks, feed, and other resources. In return, farmers raise the birds. Companies pay farmers by the pound for raised birds. The companies have a lot of power. They own the birds and tell farmers how to raise them. Sometimes companies require farmers to buy expensive equipment. This equipment may cost more than companies pay farmers for their poultry. This puts farmers in a difficult position. "They control what you do and we finally said no," farmer Karen Crutchfield said. "The cost it would have taken to update [our equipment] would have been like buying the farm again."

and turkeys that feed people across the United States. They also produce eggs. There are more than 6,500 poultry farms across the state. A quarter of all farm jobs in Arkansas are poultry farm jobs. In 2019 Arkansas produced 7.34 billion pounds (3.33 billion kg) of chicken. Most farmers raise birds for large national poultry brands. Tyson is the largest poultry company in the United States. It is based in Springdale.

Rice grows in 40 of Arkansas's 75 counties.

Arkansas is the top rice producer in the United States. Most rice farms are located in eastern Arkansas. This area has compact, wet clay soil ideal for growing rice. Soybeans, corn, and wheat are other common crops. Arkansas ranks in the top three states in the nation for cotton production. It is also a leading producer of peanuts.

Forest products are a major industry in western Arkansas. Some timber is ideal for pulpwood, which is used to make paper. Other timber is useful for lumber, utility poles, or flooring. Some people in the timber industry own the land trees grow on. Other workers harvest the trees or process them in sawmills.

TOURISM

In 2019, 36.3 million people visited Arkansas. People who like to camp, hike, bike, paddle, fish, and hunt can visit the mountains in western Arkansas. The area is also home to many cultural attractions. Fayetteville is the arts capital of Northwest Arkansas. Visitors enjoy art, music, theaters, and restaurants. In southwest Arkansas people visit Crater of Diamonds State Park. It features a field that was once the surface of a volcanic crater. Visitors search the field for rocks, gemstones, and minerals.

Eastern Arkansas attracts visitors too. The Lower Delta region is in southeast Arkansas. Visitors enjoy blues music and southern barbeque. The area also has many oxbow lakes. These U-shaped lakes are formed from bends in rivers. Lake Chicot is the largest oxbow lake in North America. With so much water in the region, waterfowl hunting is also a major attraction.

Helena, Arkansas, is known for its rich history in blues music.

OTHER INDUSTRIES

In addition to poultry and paper products, manufacturers in the state produce greeting cards, metal and rubber products, motors, and more. Once products are made, they have to be transported. Arkansas is home to 22 trucking companies, including

WALMART

Sam Walton was born in Oklahoma in 1918. After serving in World War II (1939–1945), Walton moved to Arkansas with his wife. In 1962 he opened a store called Walmart in Bentonville. The store's success grew in the next few decades. Walton opened locations all over the United States and in other countries. In 1980 Walton introduced Sam's Club, a store where members could buy items in bulk. Walton died in 1992, but his stores live on. Walmart grew to become the largest private employer in the United States. Visitors to Bentonville can learn more about the company's history at the Walmart Museum.

JB Hunt, one of the largest transport companies in North America.

Arkansas's natural resources make it a top-producing farm state. They also make it a tourist destination. They attract workers and tourists who value natural beauty, rural living, and vibrant cities.

STRAIGHT TO THE SOURCE

The King Biscuit Blues Festival is an annual showcase of blues music. It is held in Helena every October. Munnie Jordan is the executive director of the King Biscuit Blues Festival. She said:

> *This little town that we live in needs the King Biscuit Blues Festival. It's just a must for us to keep it going here in the Delta. . . . It's our culture, and we want to celebrate it. . . .*
>
> *This is where the blues started, up and down this Delta region on the Mississippi River. Memphis, Helena, Clarksdale, that's where it all started. Our stage is right on the Mississippi River. It's a permanent stage and the people sit up on the levee bank. I think they love that. It just feels good.*
>
> Source: J. D. Nash. "Festival Director Talks King Biscuit." *American Blues Scene*, 25 Sept. 2019, americanbluesscene.com. Accessed 1 June 2021.

CONSIDER YOUR AUDIENCE

Adapt this passage for a different audience, such as your principal or friends. Write a blog post conveying this same information for the new audience. How does your post differ from the original text and why?

CHAPTER FIVE

PEOPLE AND PLACES

More than 3 million people call Arkansas home. White people who are not Hispanic or Latino make up 72 percent of the state's population. Black people make up 15.7 percent. Hispanic and Latino people represent 7.8 percent, Asian Americans and Pacific Islanders 1.7 percent, and American Indians 1 percent.

CITIES AND SPORTS

Little Rock is the capital of Arkansas. It offers numerous historic and cultural sites

Little Rock is the largest city in Arkansas.

ACTIVIST AND JOURNALIST

Daisy Bates was born in Huttig in 1914. She was raised in a foster home after her mother was killed by white men. Bates and her husband moved to Little Rock, where they founded the *Arkansas State Press*. This was the state's largest Black newspaper. It was devoted to civil rights. Bates was also an activist. She was the president of the Arkansas branch of the National Association for the Advancement of Colored People (NAACP). Bates organized and mentored the Little Rock Nine. Bates drove the students to school and helped protect them from violent crowds. She continued working to help other Black people throughout her life. She was awarded the Medal of Freedom after her death in 1999.

to visit. The Clinton Presidential Library and Museum is one. Arkansan Bill Clinton was the US president from 1993 to 2001. People can also visit Little Rock Central High School National Historic Site. Students still attend the school. The National Historic Site includes a museum about the Little Rock Nine.

Fort Smith is on Arkansas's border with Oklahoma. Visitors can tour Civil War battle sites and Trail of

The University of Arkansas Razorbacks have a large following in the state. Crowds chant "Woo pig sooie" at games.

Tears milestones. Pine Bluff is southeast of Little Rock in central Arkansas. It is home to many murals celebrating the city's history. One mural features Branch Normal College, a historically Black college in Pine Bluff. It is now part of the University of Arkansas system.

Arkansas does not have any major league sports teams. But it has produced several top athletes.

Arkansan Scottie Pippen won six NBA championships with the Chicago Bulls in the 1990s. He won two Olympic gold medals as part of the US men's basketball team. NASCAR Hall of Fame driver Mark Martin is from Batesville. Arkansas is also home to one of the longest-running minor league baseball teams in the country. The Arkansas Travelers are based in Little Rock.

MUSIC IN ARKANSAS

Many important musicians in gospel music have come from Arkansas. There are different styles of gospel music. Southern gospel music has its roots in folk music. It has influenced country musicians, including Arkansas native Johnny Cash. Black gospel music blends spirituals and hymns with the blues. This genre of gospel music influenced rock and roll and pop music artists. Sister Rosetta Tharpe was a talented singer and guitar player from Arkansas. Tharpe sang gospel songs and secular music. Al Green is an Arkansan soul and gospel singer. Tharpe and Green are both in the Rock and Roll Hall of Fame.

Sister Rosetta Tharpe is called the Godmother of Rock and Roll.

Musicians get together every summer for the Fayetteville Roots Festival. Over three days, dozens of bands perform rock, blues, country, folk, and roots music. A few hours east of Fayetteville, musicians

PERSPECTIVES

FIRST FEMALE SENATOR

Hattie Caraway was the first woman elected to the US Senate. Her political career began when her husband, Senator Thaddeus Caraway, died suddenly in 1931. Arkansas's governor appointed Hattie to fill her husband's seat. Arkansans were surprised when Caraway announced she would run for the 1932 election. She told reporters, "The time has passed when a woman should be placed in a position and kept there only while someone else is being groomed for the job." She won the 1932 election and served two terms. As a senator, Caraway focused on agricultural policy. Caraway was the first woman to chair a Senate committee and the first woman to preside over the Senate.

and artists gather at the Ozark Folk Center. Visitors listen to Southern mountain music and watch artisans work. Musicians play folk songs on the fiddle, banjo, guitar, and mandolin. The fiddle is Arkansas's state instrument.

Arkansas is a state with vibrant cities. It has a thriving arts culture. Its places, people, cultures, and industry make Arkansas the Natural State.

STRAIGHT TO THE
SOURCE

Elizabeth Eckford was one of the Little Rock Nine. In an interview, she described her first attempt to attend Central High School, saying:

> *I got off the bus and I noticed along the street that there were many more cars than usual. . . . When I got to the corner where the school was, I was reassured seeing these soldiers circling the school grounds. . . . But when I stepped up [to school], [the guards] crossed rifles. . . . I approached [a] guard, [and] he directed me across the street into the crowd. It was only then that I realized that they were barring me, that I wouldn't go to school. As I stepped out into the street, the people who had been across the street started surging forward behind me.*

Source: Elizabeth Eckford. "In Her Own Words: Elizabeth Eckford." *Facing History and Ourselves*, 1997, facinghistory.org. Accessed 1 June 2021.

CHANGING MINDS

Imagine you were a student in 1957 who supported desegregating schools. How would you convince your classmates to do the same? Make sure you explain your opinion. Include facts and details that support your reasons.

IMPORTANT DATES

30,000 years ago
People first arrive in what is now Arkansas.

1541 CE
Spanish explorer Hernando de Soto is the first European to encounter American Indian peoples in the region that would become Arkansas.

1836
Arkansas becomes the twenty-fifth state on June 15.

1861
Arkansas secedes from the United States to join the Confederacy.

1868
Following the Civil War, Arkansas rejoins the United States on June 22.

1919
Hundreds of Black Arkansans are killed in the Elaine Massacre.

1957
Nine Black students enter Little Rock Central High School under the protection of US troops on September 25.

2019
36.3 million people visit Arkansas.

STOP AND THINK

Tell the Tale

Chapter One describes a journey along the Buffalo National River. Imagine you are making a similar journey. Write 200 words about the animals and plants you encounter on your trip. What do you notice as you paddle down the river?

Surprise Me

Chapter Two discusses the history of Arkansas. After reading this book, what two or three facts about Arkansas's history did you find most surprising? Write a few sentences about each fact. Why did you find each fact surprising?

Another View

This book discusses the poultry industry in Arkansas. As you know, every source is different. Ask a librarian or another adult to help you find another source about this topic. Write a short essay comparing and contrasting the new source's point of view with that of this book's author. What is the point of view of each author? How are they similar and why? How are they different and why?

Why Do I Care?

Think about what makes Arkansas special to the United States. How do resources in Arkansas affect your life? Are there places in Arkansas you would like to visit?

GLOSSARY

alluvial
relating to materials such as sand, gravel, and clay that are left behind by running water

ancestor
a family member from the past

delta
an area of low land formed by a river as it flows into another body of water

levee
a structure made from natural or human-made materials that helps keep floodwater away from people and cities during storms

perpetrator
someone who does something illegal or wrong

secede
to leave a political union

secular
not specifically religious

segregation
the separation of groups of people based on race, class, or ethnicity

tenant
someone who rents land or property from its owner

ONLINE RESOURCES

To learn more about Arkansas, visit our free resource websites below.

Visit **abdocorelibrary.com** or scan this QR code for free Common Core resources for teachers and students, including vetted activities, multimedia, and booklinks, for deeper subject comprehension.

Visit **abdobooklinks.com** or scan this QR code for free additional online weblinks for further learning. These links are routinely monitored and updated to provide the most current information available.

LEARN MORE

Harris, Duchess, and Blythe Lawrence. *Daisy Bates and the Little Rock Nine.* Abdo, 2019.

Smith, Sherri L. *What Is the Civil Rights Movement?* Penguin, 2020.

INDEX

American Indians, 5–6, 11–12, 14–15, 35, 36–37
animals, 5–6, 7, 13, 22, 23, 24, 25, 30

Bates, Daisy, 36
Buffalo River, 5–6, 9, 22
Bumpers, Dale, 7

Caraway, Hattie, 40
Cash, Johnny, 38
Civil War, 15–17, 36
Clinton, Bill, 36

Eckford, Elizabeth, 41

Fayetteville, 8, 9, 30, 39

Green, Al, 38

Helena, 9, 33
hot springs, 9, 25

ivory-billed woodpecker, 23

Jim Crow laws, 17–18
Jordan, Munnie, 33

Little Rock, 7, 9, 13, 18, 22, 35–38, 41
Little Rock Nine, 18, 36, 41

Mississippi River, 7, 9, 12, 24, 33
mountains, 9, 21–23, 24–25, 30, 40

music, 13, 30, 33, 38–40

national forests, 22, 24–25

Pine Bluff, 9, 37
poultry, 27–28

slavery, 12–17
sports, 37–38

tenant farming, 16–17
Tharpe, Sister Rosetta, 38

Walmart, 32

About the Author

A. R. Carser is a freelance writer who lives in Minnesota. She enjoys learning and writing about the history and culture of the United States.